OH MAN, ALL THIS LEGAL STUFF IS SUCH A DRAG!

Copyright © 2024, by Ron Hagelganz

All rights reserved.

979-8-89496-349-5

No portion of this book may be reproduced
in any form without written permission
from the author, except as permitted by
U.S. copyright law.

The Jesus People Coloring Trip

(not just) **FOR KIDS!**

The Jesus Movement was a powerful thing that God did in the 60's and 70's. This coloring book has drawings that look back at some highlights of that amazing time.

**Written and drawn by:
Ron Hagelganz**

special thanks to Hollis Oliver

**Digital cover work:
Andrew Alexander & Ricky Russ Jr.**

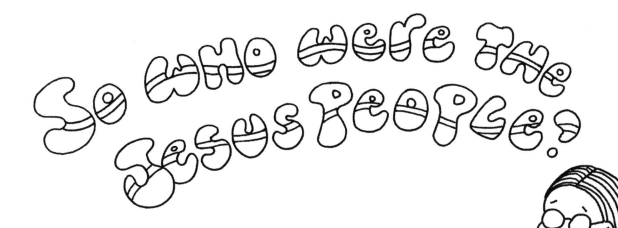

In the 60's, a lot of young people turned to the wrong things like drugs to try and find peace and happiness. But as the 70's came along, lots of them realized that they weren't really happy at all!

So many started looking for something better. That was when God started tugging at their hearts, and they began to love Jesus. And man, they *really* loved Jesus! They would tell anyone who would listen that Jesus was the way to peace, happiness, and everything they wanted.

They were often called "Jesus People!"

"Let Us In!"

As young people like Cosmo and his friends started to to find new life and hope in Jesus, they wanted to learn more about Him.

But many grown-ups in the church didn't like their long hair and bare feet, and tried to keep them away from church.

Thankfully, Pastor Chuck Smith at Calvary Chapel in Costa Mesa, CA., welcomed them in, starting what would become known as "The Jesus Movement."

"One Way"

Lots of people in the 60's and 70's would make a peace sign by pointing two fingers up.

But as they started to live for Jesus, many of them changed to just pointing one finger up. Instead of "peace", it stood for "One Way."

It meant that Jesus was the only way to find peace.

And He still is!

"Jesus Freak"

To a lot of grown-ups, the Jesus People seemed really strange. Long hair, flowers, bare feet – they just didn't get it! So some people started calling them "Jesus Freaks."

And they loved it!

*INTENTIONALLY BLANK
TO PREVENT BLEED-THROUGH*

"Broken For You"

Jesus died on the cross. And you know what? He did it willingly, because He loves us so very much, and wants to save us from our sins.

I hope you'll let Him save you, and set you free!

"Religion No – Jesus Yes!"

One thing the Jesus People rebelled against was the established religions.

The church was often stuffy, rigid and unyielding.

What we found in Jesus was not "religion", but a groovy "relationship" that changed our lives forever!

"Look Up – Jesus Is Coming"

A big deal in the Jesus Movement that I remember so clearly, is the thought of Jesus's return.

The Bible tells us that He is coming back to take us Home, and we want to be looking up, excited for Jesus to come take us to be with Him forever.

I can't wait! :)

"The Cosmo's"

Music played a huge part in the Jesus Movement.

Lots of the people who turned to Jesus were already in bands, just playing for the wrong reason.

Once Jesus got hold of their hearts, they had a new purpose and a new direction for their music, and an entirely new style of "Jesus Music" was born.

It was a beautiful thing!

"Prince of Peace"

Many people in the Jesus Movement were hippies who came out of the "summer of Love" in 1969, and were still looking for the answer for peace in their lives. And even now, it seems that what everyone really hopes for - is peace.

Well, Jesus really *is* the Prince of Peace! And as we let Him into our lives, we can have peace like we never imagined.

Sounds great doesn't it?? Well, it is!

"God Is Love"

He sure is!

And just like people found in the Jesus Movement, when you understand how much God loves you - it'll change your life forever!

"Have Jesus Will Share"

Once someone let's Jesus save them, they want to share it!

It's called "Witnessing", or telling others what Jesus has done in our lives. We wanna tell everybody! After all – someone told you right?

So who are *you* telling?

INTENTIONALLY BLANK
TO PREVENT BLEED-THROUGH

"Peace Cross"

This is a crazy drawing huh?

:)

The idea is that as the two circles overlap, the top circle shows a peace sign, and the bottom circle shows a cross.

It reminds us that the only reason we can have peace, is because of what Jesus did on the cross.

"OH MAN, LOTSA DOTS HUH?!? WELL DIG THIS: DO YOUR THING, & MAKE YOUR OWN GROOVY DESIGNS BY COLORING THE DOTS IN COOL PATTERNS OR SHAPES!"

"Jesus Saves"

An important thing that the Jesus People wanted to tell everyone was the simple truth that Jesus Saves!

He loves you, He wants to be your best friend, and help you have the very best life ever!

Have you asked Jesus to be your Savior? Do it today – there's a prayer in the back of this book if you're not sure what to do.

"Turn On"

As so many found out in the Jesus Movement, life without hope was a drag!

Nothing seemed worth living for.

But as people heard the Word of God from the Bible, believed, and "Turned On" to Jesus, everything changed!

"Oh Happy Day"

This is the title of a really popular song that came out in 1969.

It describes the joy of that day when Jesus washes our sins away, and makes us a new creation, as we give our lives to Him.

And just like for Cosmo, it's the greatest and most exciting thing that can ever happen to any of us.

Do you need that joy in your life? All ya gotta do – is ask!

INTENTIONALLY BLANK
TO PREVENT BLEED-THROUGH

"The Way, the Truth, & the Life"

Everything hinges on this!

Jesus said that **HE** is the way, the truth and the life.

And ya know what? He's either telling the Truth, or He's a liar.

What do **YOU** think?

"He Is Risen"

We're all looking for hope. We sure were back in the 70's, and it's still true today!

When Jesus rose from the dead, He proved once and for all that all of scripture is true – all the promises of God are real! And they can and will change our lives if we'll simply invite Him into our hearts.

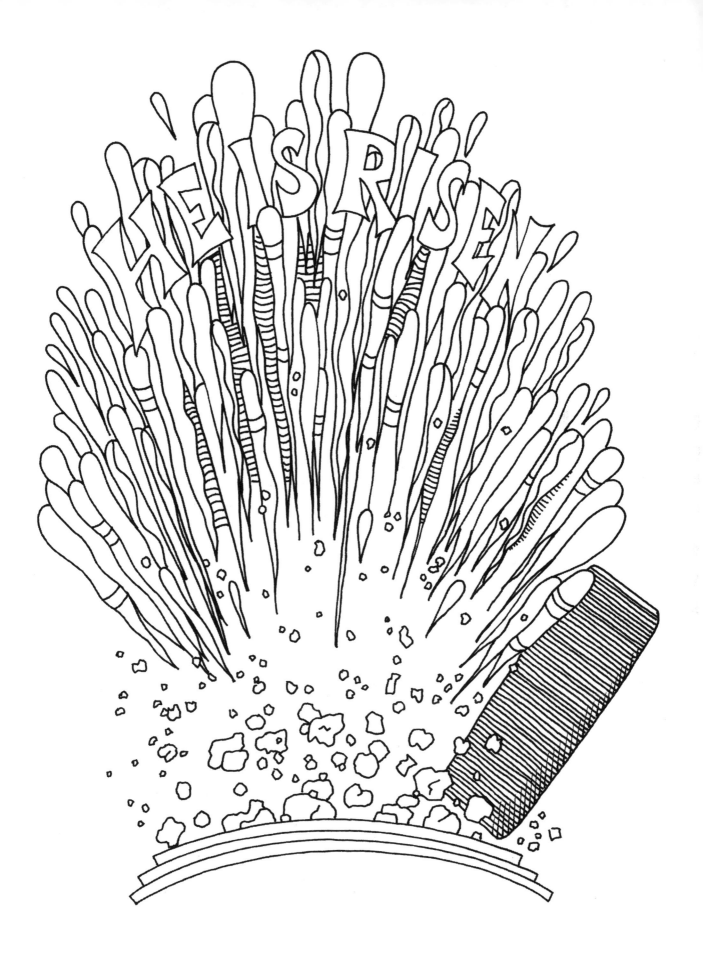

"Fishers Of Men"

As we talked about on another page, when we know Jesus, we want to tell others about Him!

But sometimes we can get nervous, or uptight about doing it.

The truth is, we never need to worry, be afraid, or get all "tangled up" in what to say - all we need to do is love Jesus, follow Him, and let His light shine through us. As we do, He'll bring along opportunities to share the Truth, and we get to go along for a very groovy ride!

"BeLIeVE"

The only way to really live, is to believe in Jesus!

And, there's more to following Jesus than just believing God's Word, we also want to live it!

The two really do go hand in hand: Believe and Live!

"Jesus Lives"

So often we get so "buddy buddy" with Jesus that we forget who He really is.

We ask Him for this and that, and often forget about Him unless we need something.

But the fact that Jesus lives, proves that He is the King of Kings, and Lord of Lords!

"One Way – His Way"

As the Jesus People found out,
the way to eternal life is really simple,
it's "One Way – His Way".

Jesus is that way, there's no other!

And as the drawing shows, the further we
get away from that truth, the fuzzier
things get.

So keep it simple, and find Life!

"The End Is Near"

An important part of the Jesus Movement was the idea that Jesus was coming back - soon!

Hal Lindsey's book "The Late Great Planet Earth" told of a world going quickly toward destruction, and many of us were convinced that "The End" was very near.

Obviously it's been 50 years or so, and Jesus hasn't come yet - but He will! And we not only want to be ready, but share Jesus with everyone we can, so they can be ready too!

I hope you enjoyed this brief look at the amazing Jesus Movement - it was really fun drawing it!

Most importantly, if God is tugging at your heart, it's because He wants to give you the gift of salvation and eternal life. He wants you to know the peace, joy, and hope that comes from knowing Jesus. And all you need to do is ask Him!

Pray a simple prayer, something like: "Jesus, I believe You are the Son of God, that You died for my sins and rose from the dead. Please forgive me for my sin and be my Lord and Savior."

Ask your parents if you need help, but it really is that simple! And if you prayed that prayer, everybody in Heaven is super excited - how groovy is that!!

God bless you with His peace!

Ron Hagelganz (and Cosmo)

Contact me: artfromthepurpledoor@gmail.com

Be sure to check out the teen/grown-up version of
"The Jesus People Coloring Trip"
by Ron Hagelganz & Hollis Oliver on Amazon!